PAUL
and the Apostles
Spread the Good News

Contemporary Bible Series
PAUL and the Apostles Spread the Good News

Published by Scandinavia Publishing House 2009
Drejervej 15,3   DK-2400 Copenhagen NV, Denmark
E-mail: info@scanpublishing.dk
Web: www.scandinavia.dk

Text copyright © Contemporary English Version
Illustrations copyright © Gustavo Mazali
Design by Ben Alex
Printed in China
ISBN 978 87 7247 684 1

PAUL
and the Apostles
Spread the Good News
Contemporary English Version

scandinavia

Contents

The Day of Pentecost

Acts 2:1-13

On the day of Pentecost all the Lord's followers were together in one place. Suddenly there was a noise from heaven like the sound of a mighty wind! It filled the house where they were meeting. Then they saw what looked like fiery tongues moving in all directions, and a tongue came and settled on each person there. The Holy Spirit took control of everyone, and they began speaking whatever languages the Spirit let them speak.

Many religious Jews from every country in the world were living in Jerusalem. And when they heard this noise, a crowd gathered. But they were surprised, because they were hearing everything in their own languages. They were excited

4

and amazed, and said, "Don't all these who are speaking come from Galilee? Then why do we hear them speaking our very own languages?"

Everyone was excited and confused. Some of them even kept asking each other, "What does all this mean?" Others made fun of the Lord's followers and said, "They are drunk."

Peter Speaks to the Crowd

1 Acts 2:14-36

Peter stood with the eleven apostles and spoke in a loud and clear voice to the crowd, "Friends and everyone else living in Jerusalem, listen carefully to what I have to say! You are wrong to think that these people are drunk. After all, it is only nine o'clock in the morning. But this is what God had the prophet Joel say, 'When the last days come, I will give my Spirit to everyone.'

Now, listen to what I have to say about Jesus from Nazareth. God proved that he sent Jesus to you by having him work miracles, wonders, and signs. All of you know this. God had already planned and decided that Jesus would be handed over to you. So you took him and had evil men put him to death on a cross. But God set him free from death and raised him to life.

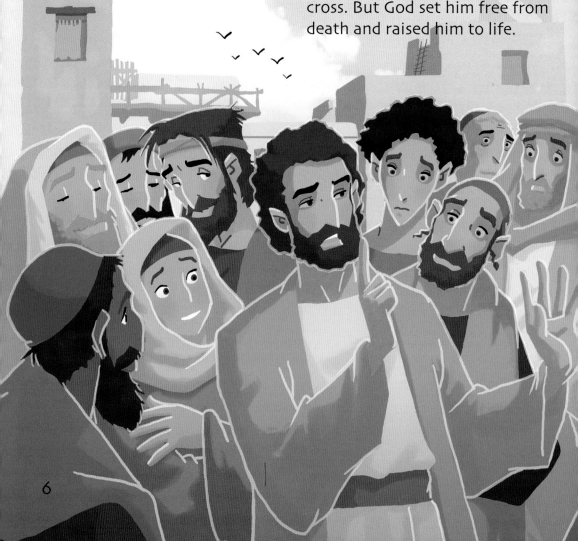

6

David knew this would happen, and so he told us that Christ would be raised to life. Jesus was taken up to sit at the right side of God, and he was given the Holy Spirit, just as the Father had promised. Jesus is also the one who has given the Spirit to us, and that is what you are now seeing and hearing. Everyone in Israel should then know for certain that God has made Jesus both Lord and Christ, even though you put him to death on a cross."

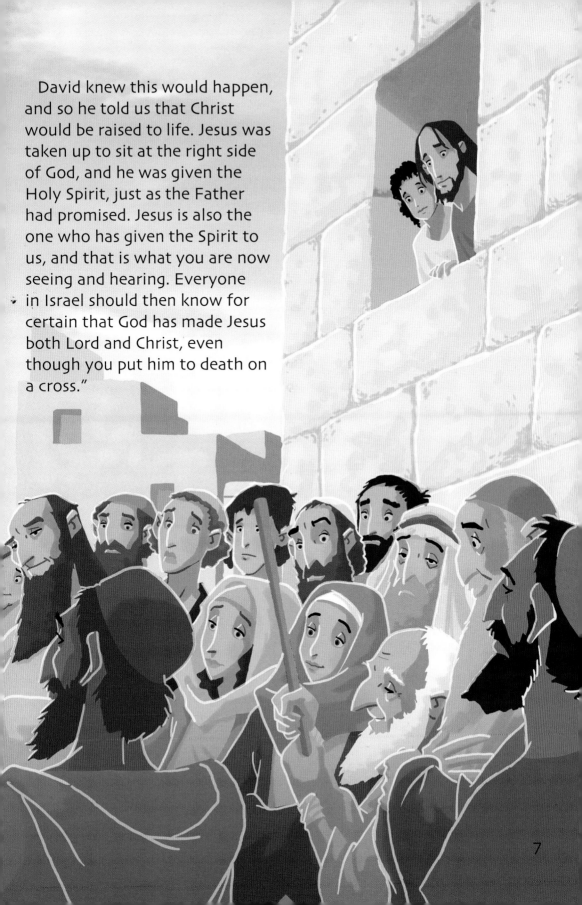

The Fellowship of the Disciples

Acts 2:37-39; 41-47

When the people heard this, they were very upset. They asked Peter and the other apostles, "Friends, what shall we do?"

Peter said, "Turn back to God! Be baptized in the name of Jesus Christ, so that your sins will be forgiven. Then you will be given the Holy Spirit. This promise is for you and your children. It is for everyone our Lord God will choose, no matter where they live."

Peter told them many other things as well. Then he said, "I beg you to save yourselves from what will happen to all these evil people."

On that day about three

thousand believed his message and were baptized. They spent their time learning from the apostles, and they were like family to each other.

Everyone was amazed by the many miracles and wonders that the apostles worked. All the Lord's followers often met together, and they shared everything they had. They would sell their property and possessions and give the money to whoever needed it. Day after day they met together in the temple. They broke bread together in different homes and shared their food happily and freely, while praising God. Everyone liked them, and each day the Lord added to their group others who were being saved.

A Lame Man Is Healed

Acts 3:1-4

The time of prayer was about three o'clock in the afternoon, and Peter and John were going into the temple. A man who had been born lame was being carried to the temple door. The man saw Peter and John entering the temple, and he asked them for money. But they looked straight at him and said, "Look up at us!" The man stared at them and thought he was going to get something. But Peter said, "I don't have any silver or gold! But I will give you what I do have. In the name of Jesus Christ from Nazareth, get up and start walking." Peter then took him by the right hand and helped him up. At once the man's feet and ankles became strong, and he jumped up and started walking. He went with Peter and John into the temple, walking and jumping and praising God.

Faith in Jesus

Acts 3:11-26

While the man kept holding on to Peter and John, the whole crowd ran to them in amazement. Peter saw that a crowd had gathered, and he said, "Friends, why are you surprised at what has happened? Why are you staring at us? Do you think we have some power of our own? Do you think we were able to make this man walk because we are so religious? The God that Abraham, Isaac, Jacob, and our other ancestors worshiped has brought honor to his Servant Jesus. He is the one you betrayed. You turned against him when he was being tried by Pilate, even though Pilate wanted to set him free.

But God raised him from death, and all of us can tell you what he has done. You see this man, and you know him. He put his faith in the name of Jesus and was made strong. Faith in Jesus made this man completely well while everyone was watching."

13

Peter and John Before the Council

Acts 4:5-20

The next morning the leaders, the elders, and the teachers of the Law of Moses met in Jerusalem. They brought in Peter and John and made them stand in the middle while they questioned them. They asked, "By what power and in whose name have you done this?"

Peter was filled with the Holy Spirit and told the nation's leaders and the elders, "You are questioning us today about a kind deed in which a crippled man was healed. But there is something we must tell you and everyone else in Israel. This man is standing here completely well because of the power of Jesus Christ from Nazareth. You put Jesus to death on a cross, but God raised him to life. Only Jesus has the power to save! His name is the only one in all the world that can save anyone."

Then the officials said to each other, "What can we do with these men? Everyone in Jerusalem knows about this miracle, and we cannot say it didn't happen." So they called the two apostles back in and told them that they must never, for any reason, teach anything about the name of Jesus.

Peter and John answered, "Do you think God wants us to obey you or to obey him? We cannot keep quiet about what we have seen and heard."

An Angel Frees the Apostles

Acts 4:32-34; 5:12-21

The group of followers all felt the same way about everything. None of them claimed that their possessions were their own, and they shared everything they had with each other. In a powerful way the apostles told everyone that the Lord Jesus was now alive. God greatly blessed his followers, and no one went in need of anything.

The apostles worked many miracles and wonders among the people. All of the Lord's followers often met in the

part of the temple known as Solomon's Porch.

Many men and women started having faith in the Lord. The high priest and all the other Sadducees who were with him became jealous. They arrested the apostles and put them in the city jail. But that night an angel from the Lord opened the doors of the jail and led the apostles out. The angel said, "Go to the temple and tell the people everything about this new life." So they went into the temple before sunrise and started teaching.

The Apostles Are Questioned
Acts 5:22-40

The high priest and his men called together their council. Then they ordered the apostles to be brought to them from the jail. The temple police returned and said, "We found the jail locked tight and the guards standing at the doors. But when we opened the doors and went in, we didn't find anyone there." Just then someone came in and said, "Right now those men you put in jail are in the temple, teaching the people!" The captain went with some of the temple police and brought the apostles back.

The high priest said to them, "We told you plainly not to teach in the name of Jesus. You have been teaching all over Jerusalem, and you are trying to blame us for his death."

Peter and the apostles replied, "We don't obey people. We obey God. You killed Jesus by nailing him to a cross. But God raised him to life and made him our Saviour. We are here to tell you about all this, and so is the Holy Spirit, who is God's gift to everyone who obeys God."

When the council members

heard this, they became so angry that they wanted to kill the apostles. But one of the members was the Pharisee Gamaliel. He said to the council, "People of Israel, be careful what you do with these men. If what they are planning is something of their own doing, it will fail. But if God is behind it, you cannot stop it anyway, unless you want to fight against God."

The council members agreed with what he said, and they called the apostles back in. They had them beaten with a whip and warned them not to speak in the name of Jesus. Then they let them go.

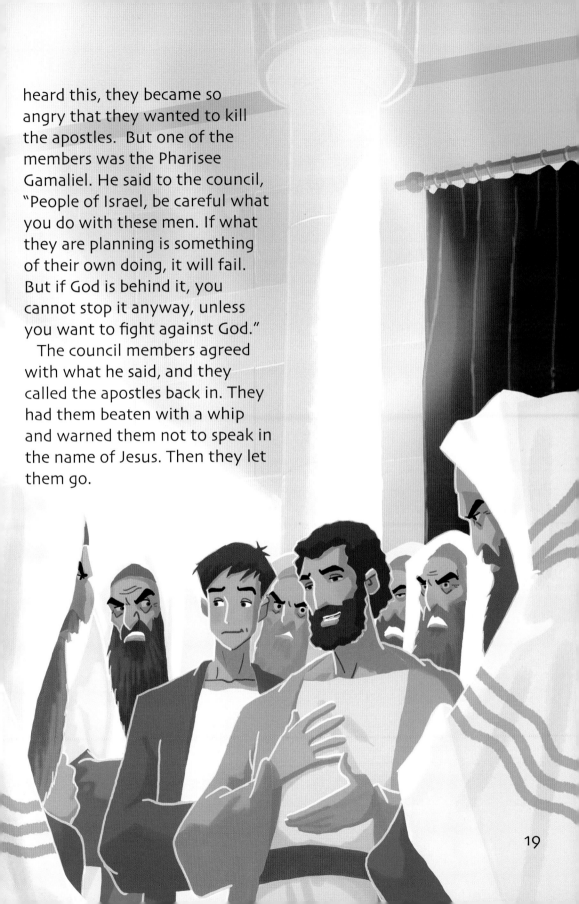

Seven Leaders for the Church

Acts 6:1-7

A lot of people were now becoming followers of the Lord. But some of the ones who spoke Greek started complaining about the ones who spoke Aramaic. They complained that the Greek-speaking widows were not given their share when the food supplies were handed out each day.

The twelve apostles called the whole group of followers together and said, "We should not give up preaching God's message in order to serve at tables. My friends, choose seven men who are respected and wise and filled with God's Spirit. We will put them in charge of these things. We can spend our time praying and serving God by preaching."

This suggestion pleased everyone, and they began by choosing Stephen. He had great faith and was filled with the Holy Spirit. Then they chose Philip, Prochorus, Nicanor, Timon, Parmenas, and also Nicolaus. These men were brought to the apostles. Then the apostles prayed and placed their hands on the men to show that they had been chosen to do this work. God's message spread, and many more people in Jerusalem became followers. Even a large number of priests put their faith in the Lord.

Stephen Is Killed

Acts 6:8-12; 7:42-53

God gave Stephen the power to work great miracles and wonders among the people. But some Jews from Cyrene and Alexandria started arguing with Stephen. But they were no match for Stephen, who spoke with the great wisdom that the Spirit gave him.

So they turned the people and their leaders and the teachers of the Law of Moses against Stephen. Then they all grabbed Stephen and dragged him in front of the council.

The high priest asked Stephen, "Are they telling the truth about you?"

Stephen answered, "You are always fighting against the Holy Spirit, just as your ancestors did. They killed the prophets who told about the coming of the One Who Obeys God. And now you have turned against him and killed him. Angels gave you God's

22

Law, but you still don't obey it."

When the council members heard Stephen's speech, they were furious. But Stephen was filled with the Holy Spirit. He looked toward heaven. Then Stephen said, "I see heaven open and the Son of Man standing at the right side of God!"

The council members shouted and covered their ears. Then they started throwing stones at him. As Stephen was being stoned to death, he called out, "Lord Jesus, please welcome me!" He knelt down and shouted, "Lord, don't blame them for what they have done." Then he died.

Saul on the Road to Damascus

Acts 8:1-4; 9:1-18

A man named Saul started making a lot of trouble for the church. He went from house to house, arresting men and women and putting them in jail. He even went to the high priest and asked for letters to the Jewish leaders in Damascus. He did this because he wanted to arrest and take to Jerusalem any man or woman who had accepted the Lord's Way.

When Saul had almost reached Damascus, a bright light from heaven suddenly flashed around him. He fell to the ground and heard a voice that said, "Saul! Saul! Why are you so cruel to me?"

"Who are you?" Saul asked.

"I am Jesus," the Lord answered. "Now get up and go into the city, where you will be told what to do."

Saul got up from the ground, and when he opened his eyes, he could not see a thing. Someone then led him by the hand to Damascus.

A follower named Ananias lived in Damascus. The Lord said to him, "Go to the house of Judas on Straight Street. When you get there, you will find a man named Saul. I have chosen him to tell foreigners, kings, and the people of Israel about me."

Ananias left and went into the house where Saul was staying. Ananias placed his hands on him and said, "Saul, the Lord Jesus has sent me. He wants you to be able to see and to be filled with the Holy Spirit."

Suddenly something like fish scales fell from Saul's eyes, and he could see. He got up and was baptized.

Peter Brings Dorcas Back to Life

Acts 9:36-43

In Joppa there was a follower named Tabitha. Her Greek name was Dorcas, which means "deer." She was always doing good things for people and had given much to the poor. But she got sick and died, and her body was washed and placed in an upstairs room.

Joppa wasn't far from Lydda, and the followers heard that Peter was there. They sent two men to say to him, "Please come with us as quickly as you can!" Right away, Peter went with them.

The men took Peter upstairs

26

into the room. Many widows were there crying. They showed him the coats and clothes that Dorcas had made while she was still alive.

After Peter had sent everyone out of the room, he knelt down and prayed. Then he turned to the body of Dorcas and said, "Tabitha, get up!" The woman opened her eyes, and when she saw Peter, she sat up. He took her by the hand and helped her to her feet.

Peter called in the widows and the other followers and showed them that Dorcas had been raised from death. Everyone in Joppa heard what had happened, and many of them put their faith in the Lord.

27

A Sheet Full of Animals

Acts 10:1-16

In Caesarea there was a man named Cornelius, who was the captain of a group of soldiers. Cornelius worshiped God, and so did everyone else who lived in his house. One afternoon, Cornelius had a vision. He saw an angel from God coming to him and calling him by name. Cornelius was surprised and stared at the angel. Then he asked, "What is this all about?"

The angel answered, "God has heard your prayers and knows about your gifts to the poor. Now send some men to Joppa for a man named Simon Peter." After saying this, the angel left.

Cornelius called in two of his servants and one of his soldiers. He explained everything to them and sent them off to Joppa.

The next day about noon these men were coming near Joppa. Peter went up on the roof of the house to pray and became very hungry. He fell sound asleep and had a vision. He saw heaven open, and something came down like a huge sheet held up by its four corners. In it were all kinds of animals, snakes, and birds. A voice said to him, "Peter, get up! Kill these and eat them."

But Peter said, "Lord, I can't do that! I've never eaten anything that is unclean and not fit to eat."

The voice spoke to him again, "When God says that something can be used for food, don't say it isn't fit to eat."

This happened three times before the sheet was suddenly taken back to heaven.

29

Peter Visits an Army Officer

Acts 10:19-45

While Peter was still thinking about the vision, the Holy Spirit said to him, "Three men are here looking for you. Hurry down and go with them. Don't worry, I sent them."

Peter went down and said to the men, "I am the one you are looking for. Why have you come?"

They answered, "Captain Cornelius sent us. He is a good man who worships God. One of God's holy angels told Cornelius to send for you, so he could hear what you have to say." Peter invited them to spend the night.

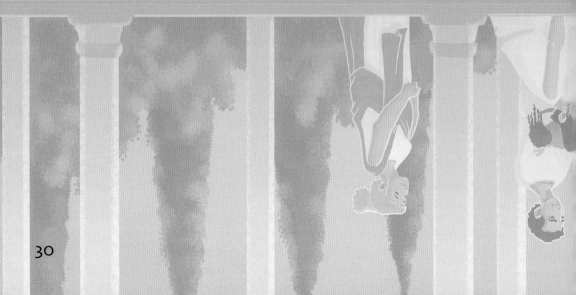

The next morning, Peter and some of the Lord's followers in Joppa left with the men who had come from Cornelius. The next day they arrived in Caesarea where Cornelius was waiting for them. He had also invited his relatives and close friends.

Peter then said, "Now I am certain that God treats all people alike. God is pleased with everyone who worships him and does right, no matter what nation they come from. This is the same message that God gave to the people of Israel, when he sent Jesus Christ."

While Peter was still speaking, the Holy Spirit took control of everyone who was listening.

Peter Is Arrested Again

Acts 12:1-8

At that time King Herod caused terrible suffering for some members of the church. He ordered soldiers to cut off the head of James, the brother of John. When Herod saw that this pleased the Jewish people, he put Peter in jail and ordered four squads of soldiers to guard him. Herod planned to put him on trial in public after the festival.

While Peter was being kept in jail, the church never stopped praying to God for him.

The night before Peter was to be put on trial, he was asleep and bound by two chains. A soldier was guarding him on each side, and two other soldiers were guarding the entrance to the jail.

Suddenly an angel from the Lord appeared, and light flashed around in the cell. The angel poked Peter in the side and woke him up. Then he said, "Quick! Get up!"

The chains fell off his hands, and the angel said, "Get dressed and put on your sandals." Peter did what he was told. Then the angel said, "Now put on your coat and follow me."

Peter Escapes from Prison

Acts 12:9-17

Peter left with the angel, but he thought everything was only a dream. They went past the two groups of soldiers, and when they came to the iron gate to the city, it opened by itself. They went out and were going along the street, when all at once the angel disappeared.

Peter now realized what had happened, and he said, "I am certain that the Lord sent his angel to rescue me from Herod and from everything the Jewish leaders planned to do to me." Then Peter went to the house of Mary the mother of John whose other name was Mark. Many of the Lord's followers had come together there and were praying.

Peter knocked on the gate, and a servant named Rhoda came to answer. When she heard Peter's voice, she was too excited to open the gate. She ran back into the house and said that Peter was standing there.

"You are crazy!" everyone told her. But she kept saying that it was Peter. Then they said, "It must be his angel." But Peter kept on knocking, until finally they opened the gate. They saw him and were completely amazed.

Peter motioned for them to keep quiet. Then he told how the Lord had led him out of jail.

Barnabas and Saul in Cyprus

Acts 13:4-12

After Barnabas and Saul had been sent by the Holy Spirit, they went to Seleucia. From there they sailed to the island of Cyprus. They arrived at Salamis and began to preach God's message. They also had John as a helper. Barnabas and Saul went all the way to the city of Paphos on the other end of the island, where they met a Jewish man named Bar-Jesus. He practiced witchcraft and was a false prophet. He also worked for Sergius Paulus, who was very smart and was the governor of the island. Sergius Paulus wanted to hear God's message, and he sent for Barnabas and Saul. But Bar-Jesus was against them. He even tried to keep the governor from having faith in the Lord.

Then Saul, better known as Paul, was filled with the Holy Spirit. He looked straight at Bar-Jesus and said, "When will you stop speaking against the true ways of the Lord? The Lord is going to punish you by making you completely blind for a while."

Suddenly the man's eyes were covered by a dark mist, and he went around trying to get someone to lead him by the hand. When the governor saw what had happened, he was amazed at this teaching about the Lord. So he put his faith in the Lord.

37

Paul and Barnabas Are Worshiped as Gods

Acts 14:8-20

In Lystra there was a man who had been born with crippled feet and had never been able to walk. The man was listening to Paul speak, when Paul saw that he had faith in Jesus and could be healed. So he looked straight at the man and shouted, "Stand up!" The man jumped up and started walking around.

When the crowd saw what Paul had done, they yelled out, "The gods have turned into humans and have come down to us!" The people then gave Barnabas the name Zeus, and they gave Paul the name Hermes, because he did the talking.

The temple of Zeus was near the entrance to the city. Its priest and the crowds wanted to offer a sacrifice to Barnabas and Paul. So the priest brought some bulls and flowers to the city gates. When the two apostles found out about this, they tore their clothes in horror and ran to the crowd, shouting, "Why are you doing this? We are humans just like you. Please give up all this foolishness. Turn to the living God, who made the sky, the earth, the sea, and everything in them."

Some Jewish leaders came and turned the crowds against Paul. They hit him with stones and dragged him out of the city, thinking he was dead. But when the Lord's followers gathered around Paul, he stood up and went back into the city.

39

Paul and Silas in Jail

Acts 16:16-24

One day we were met by a slave girl. She had a spirit in her that gave her the power to tell the future. By doing this she made a lot of money for her owners. The girl followed Paul and the rest of us and kept yelling. Finally, Paul said to the spirit, "In the name of Jesus Christ, I order you to leave this girl alone!" At once the evil spirit left her.

When the girl's owners realized that they had lost all chances for making more money, they grabbed Paul and Silas and dragged them into court. They told the officials, "These Jews are upsetting our city! They are telling us to do things we Romans are not allowed to do."

The crowd joined in the attack on Paul and Silas. Then the officials tore the clothes off the two men and ordered them to be beaten with a whip. After they had been badly beaten, they were put in jail, and the jailer was told to guard them carefully. The jailer did as he was told. He put them deep inside the jail and chained their feet to heavy blocks of wood.

Singing in Jail

Acts 16:25-34

About midnight Paul and Silas were praying and singing praises to God, while the other prisoners listened. Suddenly a strong earthquake shook the jail to its foundations. The doors opened, and the chains fell from all the prisoners.

When the jailer woke up and saw that the doors were open, he thought that the prisoners had escaped. He pulled out his sword and was about to kill himself. But Paul shouted, "Don't harm yourself! No one has escaped."

The jailer asked for a torch and went into the jail. He was shaking all over as he knelt down in front of Paul and Silas. After he had led them out of the jail, he asked, "What must I do to be saved?"

They replied, "Have faith in the Lord Jesus and you will be saved! This is also true for everyone who lives in your home."

Then Paul and Silas told him and everyone else in his house about the Lord. While it was still night, the jailer took them to a place where he could wash their cuts and bruises. Then he and everyone in his home were baptized. They were very glad that they had put their faith in God. After this, the jailer took Paul and Silas to his home and gave them something to eat.

Paul and Silas in Thessalonica

Acts 17:1-9

Paul and his friends went on to Thessalonica. A Jewish meeting place was in that city. So as usual, Paul went there to worship. He used the Scriptures to show the people that the Messiah had to suffer, but that he would rise from death. Paul also told them that Jesus is the Messiah he was preaching about. Some of them believed what Paul had said, and they became followers. Some Gentiles and many important women also believed the message.

The Jewish leaders were jealous and got some worthless bums who hung around the marketplace to start a riot in the city. They wanted to drag Paul and Silas out to the mob, and so they went straight to Jason's home. But when they did not find them there, they dragged out Jason and some of the Lord's followers. They took them to the city authorities and shouted, "Paul and Silas have been upsetting things everywhere. Now they have come here, and Jason has welcomed them into his home. All of them break the laws of the Roman Emperor by claiming that someone named Jesus is king."

The officials and the people were upset when they heard this. So they made Jason and the other followers pay bail before letting them go.

45

Paul in Athens

Acts 17:13-21

When the Jewish leaders in Thessalonica heard that Paul had been preaching God's message in Berea, they went there and caused trouble by turning the crowds against Paul.

Right away the followers sent Paul down to the coast, but Silas and Timothy stayed in Berea. Some men went with Paul as far as Athens, and then returned with instructions for Silas and Timothy to join him as soon as possible.

While Paul was waiting in Athens, he was upset to see all the idols in the city. He went to the Jewish meeting place to speak to the Jews and to anyone who worshiped with them.

Day after day he also spoke to everyone he met in the market. People were asking, "What is this know-it-all trying to say?"

Some even said, "Paul must be preaching about foreign gods! That's what he means when he talks about Jesus and about people rising from death." They brought Paul before a council called the Areopagus, and said, "Tell us what your new teaching is all about. We have heard you say some strange things, and we want to know what you mean."

More than anything else the people of Athens and the foreigners living there loved to hear and to talk about anything new.

Paul Speaks at Areopagos

Acts 17:22-34

So Paul stood up in front of the council and said,

"People of Athens, I see that you are very religious. As I was going through your city and looking at the things you worship, I found an altar with the words, 'To an Unknown God.' You worship this God, but you don't really know him. So I want to tell you about him. This God made the world and everything in it. He is Lord of heaven and earth, and he doesn't live in temples built by human hands. He doesn't need help from anyone. He gives life, breath, and everything else to all people.

God has done all this, so that we will look for him and reach out and find him. He isn't far from any of us, and he gives us the power to live, to move, and to be who we are. 'We are his children,' just as some of your poets have said.

Since we are God's children, we must not think that he is like an idol made out of gold or silver or stone. He isn't like anything that humans have thought up and made. In the past, God forgave all this because people did not know what they were doing. But now he says that everyone everywhere must turn to him. He has set a day when he will judge the world's people with fairness. And he has chosen the man Jesus to do the judging for him. God has given proof of this to all of us by raising Jesus from death."

As soon as the people heard Paul say that a man had been raised from death, some of them started laughing. Others said, "We will hear you talk about this some other time." When Paul left the council meeting, some of the men put their faith in the Lord and went with Paul.

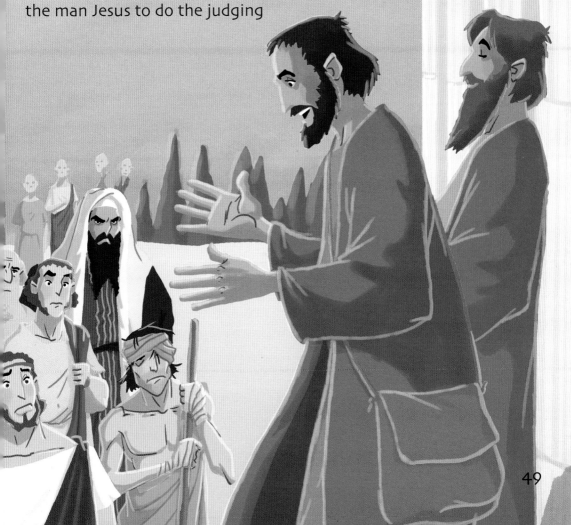

The Riot in Ephesus

Acts 19:23-30

A silversmith named Demetrius had a business that made silver models of the temple of the goddess Artemis. Those who worked for him earned a lot of money. Demetrius brought together everyone who was in the same business and said,

"Friends, you know that we make a good living at this. But you have surely seen and heard how this man Paul is upsetting a lot of people. He claims that the gods we humans make are not really gods at all. Everyone will start saying terrible things about our business. They will stop respecting the temple of

the goddess Artemis, who is worshiped in Asia and all over the world. Our great goddess will be forgotten!"

When the workers heard this, they got angry and started shouting, "Great is Artemis, the goddess of the Ephesians!" Soon the whole city was in a riot. Then everyone in the crowd rushed to the place where the town meetings were held.

Paul wanted to go out and speak to the people, but the Lord's followers would not let him. A few of the local officials were friendly to Paul, and they sent someone to warn him not to go.

Paul Is Warned

Acts 20:17-38

Paul sent a message for the church leaders at Ephesus to come and meet with him. When they got there, he said, "Some of the Jews plotted against me and caused me a lot of sorrow and trouble. But I served the Lord and was humble. When I preached in public or taught in your homes, I didn't hold back from telling anything that would help you. I told Jews and Gentiles to turn to God and have faith in our Lord Jesus.

I don't know what will happen to me in Jerusalem, but I must obey God's Spirit and go there. In every city I visit, I am told by the Holy Spirit that I will be put in jail and will be in trouble in Jerusalem. But I don't care what happens to me, as long as I finish the work that the Lord Jesus gave me to do. And that work is to tell the good news about God's great kindness."

After Paul had finished speaking, he knelt down with all of them and prayed. Everyone cried and hugged and kissed him. They were especially sad because Paul had told them, "You will never see me again."

Then they went with him to the ship.

A Mob Turns Against Paul

Acts 21:27-36; 22:23-24

Some of the Jewish people from Asia saw Paul in the temple. They got a large crowd together and started attacking him. They were shouting, "Friends, help us! This man goes around everywhere, saying bad things about our nation and about the Law of Moses and about this temple. He has even brought shame to this holy temple by bringing in Gentiles."

The whole city was in an uproar, and the people turned into a mob. They grabbed Paul and dragged him out of the temple. Then suddenly the doors were shut.

The people were about to kill Paul when the Roman army commander heard that all Jerusalem was starting to riot.

So he quickly took some soldiers and officers and ran to where the crowd had gathered. The army commander went over and arrested Paul and had him bound with two chains. Then he tried to find out who Paul was and what he had done. Part of the crowd shouted one thing, and part of them shouted something else. But they were making so much noise that the commander could not find out a thing. Then he ordered Paul to be taken into the fortress. As they reached the steps, the crowd became so wild that the soldiers had to lift Paul up and carry him. The crowd followed and kept shouting, "Kill him! Kill him!"

The Roman commander ordered Paul to be taken into the fortress and beaten with a whip.

Paul Speaks Before the Governor

Acts 24:24-27; 25:8-12

Felix the governor and his wife Drusilla went to the place where Paul was kept under guard. They sent for Paul and listened while he spoke to them about having faith in Christ Jesus. But Felix was frightened when Paul started talking to them about doing right, about self-control, and about the coming judgment. So he said to Paul, "That's enough for now. You may go. But when I have time I will send for you." After this, Felix often sent for Paul and talked with him, because he hoped that Paul would offer him a bribe.

Two years later Porcius Festus became governor in place of Felix.

Then Paul spoke in his own defense, "I have not broken the Law of my people. And I have not done anything against either the temple or the Emperor."

Festus wanted to please the leaders. So he asked Paul, "Are you willing to go to Jerusalem and be tried by me on these charges?" Paul replied, "I am on trial in the Emperor's court, and that's where I should be tried. You know very well that I have not done anything to harm the Jewish nation. If I had done something deserving death, I would not ask to escape the death penalty. But I am not guilty of any of these crimes. I now ask to be tried by the Emperor himself."

After Festus had talked this over with members of his council, he told Paul, "You have asked to be tried by the Emperor, and to the Emperor you will go!"

Heading for Rome

Acts 27

Then it was time for us to sail to Rome. We sailed along slowly for several days. But soon a strong wind blew against us from the island. The wind struck the ship, and we could not sail against it. So we let the wind carry the ship. For fourteen days and nights we had been blown around over the Mediterranean Sea. But about midnight the sailors realized that we were getting near land. The sailors were afraid that we might hit some rocks, and they let down four anchors from the back of the ship. Then they prayed for daylight.

Morning came, and the ship's crew saw a coast that they did not recognize. But they did see a cove with a beach. So they decided to try to run the ship aground on the beach. They cut the anchors loose and let them sink into the sea. At the same time they untied the ropes that were holding the rudders. Next, they raised the sail at the front of the ship and let the wind carry the ship toward the beach. But it ran aground on a sandbank. The front of the ship stuck firmly in the sand, and the rear was being smashed by the force of the waves. Captain Julius ordered everyone who could swim to dive into the water and head for shore. Then he told the others to hold on to planks of wood or parts of the ship. At last, everyone safely reached shore.

Rome at Last

Acts 28:1-10; 11-31

When we came ashore, we learned that the island was called Malta. The local people were very friendly, and they welcomed us by building a fire, because it was rainy and cold.

After Paul had gathered some wood and had put it on the fire, the heat caused a snake to crawl out, and it bit him on the hand.

Paul shook the snake off into the fire and wasn't harmed. The people kept thinking that Paul would either swell up or suddenly drop dead. They watched him for a long time, and when nothing happened to him, they said, "This man is a god."

Everyone on the island brought their sick people to Paul, and they were all healed. The people were very respectful to us, and when we sailed, they gave us everything we needed. Three months later we sailed in a ship that had been docked at Malta for the winter. We arrived in Rome, and Paul was allowed to live in a house by himself with a soldier to guard him. Paul called together some of the Jewish leaders. Many of them came to his house. From early morning until late in the afternoon, Paul talked to them about God's kingdom.

For two years Paul stayed in a rented house and welcomed everyone who came to see him. He bravely preached about God's kingdom and taught about the Lord Jesus Christ, and no one tried to stop him.

The Contemporary Bible Series